The Definitive Guide to
UNDERGROUND
HUMOR

Unearthed and Edited by
Edward Bergin

NON SEQUITUR By Wiley

© 1994, Washington Post Writers Group. Reprinted with permission.

Published by: OFFbeat Publishing
P.O. Box 735
Waterbury, CT 06720-0735

Copyright © 1995 and 1996 by Edward Bergin
First Printing—November 1995
Second Printing—August 1996, revised
PRINTED IN THE UNITED STATES OF AMERICA

Certain quotations in this book come from the following sources: *Peter's Quotations,* ©1977 by Dr. Laurence J. Peter, William Morrow & Co., Inc.; *The Concise Columbia Dictionary of Quotations,* ©1989 by Robert Andrews, Avon Books; *The Comedy Quote Dictionary,* ©1992 by Ronald L. Smith, Doubleday Books; *Bartlett's Familiar Quotations* by John Bartlett, Justin Kaplan, general editor, ©1992 by Little, Brown & Co.; *Comedians' Quote Book* by Merrit Malloy and Marsha Rose, ©1993 by Porosan Group, Sterling Publishing Company, Inc.; *Speaker's Sourcebook II* by Glenn Van Ekeren, ©1994 by Prentice Hall. Certain quotes are from Correct Quotes. Copyright ©1992 by WordStar International, Inc. WordStar International, Inc. is a registered trademark of SoftKey, Inc.

Certain headstone epitaphs in this book come from the following sources: *A Selection of Sepulchral Curiosities,* ©1823 by T. Kinnersley, published by T. Kinnersley, New York; *A Collection of Curious and Interesting Epitaphs,* ©1869 by Frederick Teague Cansick, printed by Plackett and Moody S. Bride's Press, London; *A Book of Epitaphs, Amusing Curious and Quaint,* ©1873 by Charles Northend, printed by G.W. Carleton and Co., Publishers, New York; *Funny Epitaphs,* ©1900 by Arthur Wentworth Eaton, printed by the Mutual Book Company, Boston; *Here Lies: Being A Collection of Ancient and Modern, Humorous and Queer Inscriptions From Tombstones,* ©1902 by W.H. Howe, printed for the New Amsterdam Book Company.

Publisher's Cataloging-in-Publication Data
Bergin, Edward, 1965 -
The Definitive Guide to Underground Humor / edited by Edward Bergin.
2nd ed., revised
1. Quotations—Humor.   I. Title.
2. Undertakers and undertaking—Anecdotes, facetiae, etc.
3. Funeral homes—Anecdotes, facetiae, etc.
4. Funeral rites and ceremonies—Anecdotes, facetiae, etc.
5. Epitaphs—Humor.
PN6231.D35   1995   818.5402
Library of Congress Catalog Card Number: 95-74710
ISBN 0-9648442-8-1: $8.95 Softcover

Contents

This book is dedicated to Tom, a good friend of mine whose wonderfully morbid sense of humor inspired the creation of this book.

Acknowledgments

I would like to take this opportunity to thank all of the funeral directors, embalmers, pall bearers, and other funeral-related workers from around the United States who took time out of their hectic schedules to share their humorous experiences with me. Without their help and encouragement, this book would have never materialized. I offered to thank each of them by name, but for some strange reason none of them wanted their names revealed anywhere in my book. Hmmm. I wonder why . . .

Also, I'd like to thank the following cartoonists and/or their syndicates for granting me permission to reprint the funeral-flavored comic strips contained in my book: Wiley Miller and The Washington Post Writers Group (especially Permissions Editor Kim Arrington) for the *Non Sequitur* strips; Johnny Hart (especially Perri Hart) and Creators Syndicate, Inc., for *The Wizard of Id* strips.

My deepest appreciation goes to all of my friends and family members who proofed this book for me: Ginger, Shyla, Mary Margaret, Aunt Maggie and Aunt Liz (my "older sister" who—no matter how old I am—will always be 10 years older than me!).

Special thanks to everyone who wittingly or unwittingly had a hand in helping me put this book together: author John Guevin for providing me with the information on how to do it myself; Ruth Russell, of the Silas Bronson Library, for telling me what all those jumbled numbers and letters mean on a book's title page and for figuring out the right combinations to include on *my* title page; William J. Bergin Sr. for his fantastic illustration of an old-time funeral director; Kate and Lisa, of Outback Computer Graphics, for helping me to finalize the book's front and back covers; and Sherry Sanderson, of McNaughton & Gunn, Inc., for her efforts and patience during the course of getting this book printed.

Finally, I owe an immense debt of gratitude to stand up comedian/writer Anita Wise for taking time out of her busy schedule to relate to me her humorous quotes about death and for writing such an apropos Foreword to my book. I hope you screw up many, many manicures before you finally get that good one. Thanks for everything, Anita!

Foreword

by

Anita Wise,
Stand Up Comedian/Writer

RING AROUND THE ROSY

Edmund Gwenn, the famous actor, observed "Dying is easy. Comedy is difficult." Well, any comic will tell you, comedy about dying is *really* hard. But necessary. For what greater triumph of the human spirit exists than to defiantly mock the grinning reaper, specter of our darkest fears? "Hey, Death—is that a sickle in your hand or are you just glad to see me?"

Because dying and the business of death is carried out by humans, there will be comedy in it, though it is considered bad form in most of the attendant activities to react to it or even acknowledge its presence. Hence this book. In its pages feel free to revel in the lighter side of the most equal opportunity affliction after taxes. Don't feel guilty; sooner or later, everybody's going to get their turn. Except me. To those who might find the concept unseemly, ponder this: we enter the world crying, isn't it only fitting to leave it laughing? After all, death is not the final exit, but only a revolving door.

Laugh in Peace.

Anita Wise is a stand up comedian/writer who has appeared on the "Tonight Show" & "Seinfeld" and writes a monthly column for Kinesis *magazine. She intends to never die . . . again.*

Quaint
Quotes

THE WIZARD OF ID   Brant parker and Johnny hart

I don't want to achieve immortality through my
work . . . I want to achieve it through not dying.
— *Woody Allen*

Forest Lawn is like a Disneyland for shut-ins.
— *Jack Parr*

In the Jewish religion, we bury our dead before the
next sunset. Which is civilized. They ain't
going to get no better.
— *Alan King*

I never wanted to see anybody die, but there are a
few obituary notices I have read with pleasure.
— *Clarence Darrow*

If, after I depart this vale, you ever remember me
and have thought to please my ghost, forgive some
sinner and wink your eye at some homely girl.
— *H.L. Mencken*

Everyone is afraid of dying alone. I don't
understand. Who wants to die and have
to be polite at the same time?
— *Quentin Crisp*

How can I die? I'm booked!
— *George Burns*

I'm not afraid of dying. It'll be the one
manicure I don't screw up.
— *Anita Wise*

I think the easiest job in the world has to be
coroner. Surgery on dead people. What's the
worst thing that could happen? If everything
went wrong, maybe you'd get a pulse.
— *Dennis Miller*

Dropping dead is still the largest cause
of death in our society.
— *Anonymous*

The great thing about suicide is that it's not one of
those things you have to do now or you'll lose your
chance. I mean, you can always do it later.
— *Harvey Fierstein*

On the plus side, death is one of the few things
that can be done as easily lying down.
— *Woody Allen*

For three days after death, hair and fingernails
continue to grow but phone calls taper off.
— *Johnny Carson*

We pay for the mistakes of our ancestors, and it
seems only fair that they should leave us
the money to pay with.
— *Don Marquis*

Eternal rest sounds comforting in the pulpit; well,
you try it once, and see how heavy
time will hang on your hands.
— *Mark Twain*

My Uncle Pat, every morning he reads the death
column in the paper. And he can't understand
how people always die in alphabetical order.
— *Hal Roach*

I'm not afraid of death. It's the make-over at the
undertaker's that scares me . . . They try to make
you look as lifelike as possible, which defeats the
whole purpose. It's hard to feel bad for somebody
who looks better than you do.
— *Anita Wise*

If there is no Hell, a good many preachers are obtaining money under false pretenses.
— *William A. Sunday*

To get to Heaven, turn right and keep straight.
— *Anonymous*

Death is a very dull, dreary affair, and my advice to you is to have nothing whatever to do with it.
— *W. Somerset Maugham*

The chief problem about death, incidentally, is the fear that there may be no afterlife—a depressing thought, particularly for those who have bothered to shave. Also, there is the fear that there is an afterlife but no one will know where it's being held.
— *Woody Allen*

If I could drop dead right now, I'd be the happiest man alive!
— *Samuel Goldwyn*

Dying is easy. Comedy is difficult.
— *Edmund Gwenn*

Death is nature's way of saying,
"Your table is ready."
— *Robin Williams*

Either he's dead or my watch has stopped.
— *Groucho Marx*

People always say "He died penniless," as if it's a
terrible thing. Sounds like good timing to me.
— *Al Cleathen*

She made a ravishing corpse.
— *Ronald Firbank*

They say that Hell is hot, but is it humid? Because
I can take the heat; it's the humidity I can't stand.
— *Ronnie Shakes*

Ridiculous Removals & Funeral Arrangements

THE WIZARD OF ID

Brant parker and Johnny hart

Don't Wake Me . . . I'm Only Sleeping

My partner and I went to a house to remove the body of a man who had died in bed. His bedroom contained two daybeds opposite one another. So when we saw a body lying on the closer of the two beds, we figured it was the deceased.

But as we were lowering the body into the carrier, the deceased's son came into the room and suddenly informed us, "You've got the wrong body. That's my mother. My father is in the *other* bed!"

We took the mother out of the carrier and put her back into her bed.

Amazingly, she slept through the whole thing.

Payback Is A Bitch

A woman came into my funeral home to make the arrangements for her recently deceased husband, but all she did was complain about him. This woman made it very clear to me from the beginning that she had hated her husband. She kept referring to him as "that womanizing bastard."

When I asked where she planned on burying her late husband, she surprised me by telling me that she was going to bury him on top of her mother in her mother's grave. She said that her mother's grave was double-depth and it shouldn't be a problem.

Still, I was puzzled by her request and asked, "If you hated your husband so much, why would you want to bury him with your mother?"

"It would be poetic justice," she informed me. "My husband hated my mother and what better way to get back at him than to stick him in the ground with her. She can nag him for all of eternity!"

False Teeth And False Alarm

Back in the days before there were ambulances and ambulance services, funeral homes were often called upon to take sick people to hospitals in their hearses. A friend of mine had a funny story about someone his funeral home had taken to the hospital.

My friend was at his funeral home when he received a call from a man who said he needed to take his father to the hospital. The son said his father was close to dying, and he wanted to make sure his father's final hours alive would be comfortable ones. My friend told the son he would send a couple of men over right away to take them to the hospital, and then he hung up the phone.

During the ride, the son told the two men that their funeral home was the one his father wanted to go to when he died. He then reached into his pocket and handed them his father's false teeth, saying his father wanted them put in his mouth for his funeral.

The two men dropped off the sick man and his son at the hospital and took the dentures back to the funeral home.

However, the false teeth were never put into

the father's mouth for his funeral service because the service never happened. Several weeks went by and my friend never heard from the son again.

My friend remained in the dark about the status of the dying father until an old man walked into his funeral home two months later and asked him, "Hey, have you got Joe Smith's teeth here?"

"Yeah," he said. "They're in the prep room. Let me go get them."

When my friend returned with the false teeth, the old man took them, put them in his mouth and walked out the door.

Kick Or Treat

In the fall—sometime in late October or early November—a woman walked into my funeral home and said she wanted to make funeral arrangements for her recently deceased husband.

During the course of getting the preliminary information from this woman, she told me that her husband had died at home. She had been cleaning the windows in her house when she looked outside and noticed something in a pile of leaves in the backyard. So she went out to investigate and found something that looked like a body lying in the leaves.

She then gave it a few swift kicks with her foot because, as she put it to me, "You know how around Halloween kids like to stuff old clothes full of leaves and put them outside to make you think that it's somebody? But when I came around to the other side to have a look, it wasn't a prank at all. It was my husband!"

Diagnosis: Brief Illness

As a rule, our funeral home doesn't give out any personal information about the people we are burying. This particularly holds true in cases of suicide and other kinds of death that are sensitive in nature. We feel it might add to a family's grief by airing their dirty laundry in public. So when we write the obituary for the newspaper or when people call to inquire about the cause of death, we usually state that the person died after a brief illness.

But being so vague did get us into trouble once.

We had a case where we received a call to make the funeral arrangements for a man who had just been killed in a factory accident. When I called the local newspaper to give them all the funeral and personal information for his obituary notice, I stated that this man had died after a brief illness.

The next day, the editor of the paper phoned the funeral home and proceeded to call me every nasty name in the book.

"Why are you swearing at me?" I asked him.

"Why? Because of what you put as the cause of death in that factory worker's obituary," he said. He informed me he'd just read a front page article in his newspaper which revealed that the real cause of death had been from having a ten ton machine drop on top of him. "How could you possibly put in his obit that he 'died after a brief illness?'"

I replied, "I'm no doctor, but it looked brief to me!"

Drop Your Drawers, But Not The Body

During a period in my life when I was seriously trying to lose some weight, I received a call to make a removal at an apartment complex on the other side of town. Because nobody else was around at the funeral home to help me except for Sally, our female funeral director, I was forced into taking her with me.

When we arrived at the complex, the police officer at the scene said the deceased had died in a basement apartment, but that there shouldn't be any problems getting the body out. He explained to us that before our funeral home had been called, an ambulance company had been called first. They had taken their stretcher down into and then back out of the apartment when they realized their services weren't needed.

The officer also said that the deceased was a ninety-year-old woman, so I assumed she was a little old lady. That being the case, there definitely wouldn't be any problem getting the stretcher out with her on it. We'd go straight in and straight back out. No big deal.

As Sally went to get the stretcher out of the car,

I went to have a look at the little old lady.

However, the old lady I found in the basement apartment was anything *but* little. She was a ninety-year-old woman who tipped the scales at 280 pounds, and whose rear-end was nearly the size of Rhode Island!

Although I had been trying out a number of different diets at the time, I was still roughly the same large proportions as this woman. I figured we'd still be able to get her out if I got behind the stretcher and put my weight into pushing it up the stairs.

Everything was going smoothly, too, until we got halfway up. At that point, I realized I must've hit upon a diet that was working for me because my pants suddenly let go from my waist and dropped down to my ankles!

"Hold on a minute," I whispered quietly to Sally, trying to get her to stop.

"Just keep going," she replied. "We've only got two more to go."

I told her in a much louder whisper, "Stop pulling the stretcher and get down here."

"What's the problem?"

"Just get down here . . . *now!*"

Finally, she came down a couple of steps, took one look at me standing there in my white underwear and black socks and started laughing uncontrollably. Her laughter got even louder as she held onto the back of the stretcher for me while I pulled my pants back up.

I was half-expecting the family to walk through the door, wondering what the hell we were doing to their mother, so I asked her to control herself.

We made it to the station wagon and loaded the deceased before she became overwhelmed by another fit of laughter. This caused me to start laughing, too, and the two of us fell against the back of the wagon as we thought about what had occurred inside.

We were still roaring in laughter when we both happened to notice two old ladies looking at us from another apartment in the complex. These old women were shaking their heads in disbelief, appalled by our seemingly blasphemous behavior.

I think it's a safe bet that our funeral home won't get the call to bury either one of them.

This Job Is For The Birds

My boss and I went to make the removal of a very prominent man in town. After we got to the house, I waited outside in the hearse while he went in to get the obituary information from the widow.

He was only in there a short time before he came out and told me that he wanted me to go inside with him. I assumed he wanted me to go because the body was ready to be removed, so I started following him with the carrier. But he stopped me, saying, "No. Don't bring the carrier. Just come inside and sit with me."

As I sat with my boss and the widow while they discussed all the information that was to be included in the obituary, I began to wonder why he wanted me inside the house with him.

However, the reason suddenly became very clear when the family's pet bird flew downstairs and perched on top of my boss's head. He was deathly afraid of animals and wanted me in there for moral support.

A Real Couch Potato

Preparing to make a removal from a fifth floor apartment, I went upstairs first to assess the situation. I found the family in the kitchen, and they told me that their father had passed away on the living room couch. I took a quick look at the deceased, talked to the family again for a minute and decided that it would be best to remove him before getting the obituary information. So I went down to get my partner and the carrier.

On the way back upstairs, my partner was wondering if this was going to be an easy removal and asked me if the father was a large man.

I said, "It didn't look like he was very big. He had a blanket draped over him, but it didn't look like there was much underneath it."

But when we reached the living room, put the carrier down on the floor and took the blanket off this man, we both nearly went into shock. There weren't any cushions on the couch—that was all him! He weighed between 350 and 370 pounds.

Needless to say, he was so heavy that the two of us couldn't carry him down the stairs. We had to drag him down four flights to get him out.

Sick-gars . . . Cigarettes

In the middle of a particularly long and hot summer, my brother and I went to remove a dead body from a seventh floor walkup apartment.

The state medical examiner greeted us on the first floor porch, and I asked him about the condition of the deceased.

"Let's put it this way," the good doctor said. "I've pronounced him dead from here."

I knew the body must smell really bad if the doctor had been able to pronounce this person dead from the first floor of a seven floor apartment building, so I suggested to my brother that we should get some kind of spray to kill the odor.

But my brother—who had become quite cocky after having done removals for a number of years— said, "Forget the spray. I'll get a cigar and smoke it on the way up. That'll kill any smell."

He went to a nearby store, bought a cigar and came right back.

My brother lit up on the first floor, but he never found out if the cigar smoke would kill the smell because it nearly killed him first. By the time we reached the third floor, he'd turned positively green from smoking and had to go back downstairs to get some fresh air.

I had to get some spray and a policeman to help me make the removal.

Just The Facts, Ma'am

Our funeral home got a call asking us to handle the funeral for a woman who had just died. I knew the deceased's sister, Nancy, so I decided to go over to Nancy's apartment to get the obituary information and to discuss the particulars of her sister's funeral service with her.

I knocked on Nancy's door and when she opened it, I was startled to find her standing in the doorway without a stitch of clothing on. She was completely naked.

I knew this woman, but I didn't know her *that* well. I said to her, "Go put some clothes on!"

Nancy came back a few minutes later wearing a housecoat, and she led me through her apartment until we reached the dining room. We both sat down at the table and started going over all the information she wanted to include in the obituary notice.

I couldn't help but notice Nancy's housecoat as I talked with her, and looking at it made me wonder what she had been doing before that would have distracted her enough to answer the door in only her birthday suit. But when some man suddenly started yelling to Nancy from another room in the apartment, I soon discovered what the majority of her attention had been focused on.

I turned and looked over from the dining room into a bedroom and saw this man lying naked on a bed. He was yelling for Nancy to come back and finish fooling around with him.

Right Name, Wrong Address

Our answering service received a call asking for our funeral home to make the removal of a—let's say—Michael Smith. A member of the deceased's family gave them the location of the deceased and the telephone number where the family could be reached. After taking down the information, the service called to tell me about it.

I called the family right back and talked to the daughter, Margaret, who acknowledged her father had just died. I asked her if the doctor had been there yet to pronounce her father dead, and she said that he was on his way. I told her I would also be there shortly.

I grabbed two men from the funeral home to help me make the removal, and we left to go to the house.

Now, I knew the family of a Michael Smith and had even gone to high school with the daughter, Margaret, so I never bothered to verify the address of the deceased. However, I quickly realized upon arriving at the Smith house that I should've asked for the address.

While the two men waited in the station wagon, I walked up to the front door and rang the doorbell. After a few seconds, the man I thought I was supposed to be removing unexpectedly answered the door.

I was shocked by the sight of him still alive and stammered, "Uh, Mike, h-how are you doing?"

"I'm doing great. What's going on?" he asked.

I said, "Well, there seems to be a mistake."

He looked over, saw the station wagon sitting in his driveway and said, "You're right about that. Nobody's dead here!"

He let me inside his house to call the answering service back, and I got the correct address.

It turned out to be a wacky coincidence where the deceased had the same name as the man I knew, and each of them had a daughter named Margaret.

When I got back to the station wagon, one of the guys asked me, "What the heck are we doing at this house?"

"We are just out sightseeing," I said totally deadpan. "I wanted to see an old friend of mine."

What? No Medal For Bravery?

My partner and I went to do the removal of a man who had died after shooting himself in the head with a small pistol. We found the deceased in his bed with the gun still pressed against his head.

A police officer entered the room, saw us getting ready to move this man and shouted, "Oh, Jesus. Whatever you do, don't touch him. That gun is still loaded! There's a bullet half-in and half-out of the chamber."

But my partner didn't listen.

Without any warning, he suddenly reached over and did something to the gun, causing the bullet to eject harmlessly into the air and emptying the gun's chamber.

My partner was very proud of himself until I sized up the situation by informing him, "Yeah, you're a real hero. You just disarmed a dead man."

From Pushing Up Petals To Pushing Down Pedals

A family came into my friend's funeral home to make funeral arrangements for their deathly ill mother—she wasn't expected to make it through the night. Since it was already Friday night and they didn't expect her to live longer than early Saturday morning, the family made tentative plans to have the waking hours on Sunday and the funeral on Monday.

As they were leaving, the family told my friend that he should expect to receive a call from them very shortly to go get their mother's body from the hospital. It would probably be only a matter of hours.

However, the night came and went with no phone call from the family.

Saturday came and nothing happened.

The weekend passed and still no call.

The next time my friend heard from or saw anyone from that family again, it was the near-death mother. He watched in amazement as she rode by the front of his funeral home on a bicycle.

He Thud He Heard A Noise

A man's twin brother had died at home with him, and we arrived at the house to find the living twin standing next to his brother's dead body.

My partner asked him, "What happened, Freddy?"

Freddy plainly replied, "Oh, I don't know. All I heard was an awful thud."

He's Not Just The President, He's Also A Client

While working on a ladder in his backyard patio, a gentleman who was the president of a very well-known company in town had a heart attack and died. Our funeral home got the call from the family to handle the funeral, so my partner and I went out to the house to make the removal.

The first thing we did when we got to the house was to take off the sheet covering him to get a better look at the condition of his body. It first appeared that this man had fallen off the ladder and landed on his head because the front part of his scalp was flapping way back on the top of his head. But because the family was in the house, we didn't have time to look at him thoroughly.

We quickly put him in a pouch, onto our carrier, loaded him into the hearse and left.

Back at the funeral home, we immediately brought him into the embalming room, took him out of the pouch and put him on the table. We needed to start working on this man right away if we were going to get his head in shape for his wake.

Taking a closer look, however, we discovered that this man didn't have a hair on his head—he was a real cue-ball! The patch of hair that had been flapping on top of his head at his house was the front of his toupee, which had somehow come undone during his death.

Help! I've Fallen, And I Can't Get Up!

One time a friend of mine went alone to a hospice to make a removal, which is never a wise idea because you never know what might happen while taking the body back to the funeral home. My friend, unfortunately, had to learn this lesson the hard way.

While he was taking the body back to the hearse, the stretcher started to tip and he tried to stop it from going over. But he only weighed 140 pounds and could do little to stop the momentum of the 250 pound body.

The stretcher landed on top of him and he was pinned underneath it in the parking lot for almost twenty minutes.

Luckily, a couple of security guards finally heard him yelling for help, or he might've been stuck out there all night.

Do You Want That Removal With Or Without Eggs?

Late one evening, a woman's husband died at home, so my partner and I went out to the house to make the removal. He went inside to talk to the widow while I waited in the hearse until he was ready to get the body.

After a few minutes, he came back to the hearse carrying two cartons of eggs—a dozen eggs in each carton. I watched him as he opened the passenger's side door and placed the two cartons on the seat.

He looked all out of sorts, like his feathers had really been ruffled, so I asked, "What's the story with the eggs?"

He said to me, "It's a long story. I'll tell you about it after we make the removal."

As we were carrying the deceased out of the house, I was curious to hear what had happened before and asked him again about the eggs.

He said that during his conversation with the

widow, she had asked him if he thought his wife could use some eggs. He figured she wanted to get rid of the eggs because they were due to go bad during the three day span of her husband's funeral. So my cheap partner—Mr. Anything for Free—had said "yes." And when she'd asked him if his wife could use a couple dozen, he guessed she could. He figured he'd give the other dozen to me.

The widow went outside to the hen house in her backyard to get the eggs.

When she came back inside, she handed him the cartons and threw him for quite a loop by telling him, "That'll be $1.75."

How Much Is That Car—I Mean—That Casket?

I was in our display room trying to help a member of the deceased's family pick out a casket. This is usually a simple task. But it became a monumental undertaking because this man turned out to be a real cheapskate, making me explain the cost of every casket I showed him.

At one point, he was questioning me about the price of two metal caskets that were very similar in looks but very different in price.

"The higher priced casket has a bed in it and the cheaper one doesn't," I informed him. "That's why there's a difference in price."

But he said, "Hey, that doesn't really make a

difference to me. I don't care whether it has a bed in it or not. What else has it got?"

Irritated and frustrated in having to deal with such a cheap man, I quipped, "Power steering."

He didn't hassle me again.

Summer's The Season For Hanging Outside

One really hot summer night, I got a call from the police asking me to make a removal. They told me the man had died while trying to hang himself at his fourth floor apartment.

I arrived at the scene and was just about ready to go up to the apartment with the carrier when a police officer asked me where I was going.

"I'm going up to get him," I replied.

"Don't bother. He's right over there," the officer said, pointing to some bushes. "It was so hot inside his apartment he must've decided he wanted to hang himself someplace cooler. Unfortunately, the rope on his porch broke and he died from the fall."

The Water Was Cold . . . And Deep, Too

While making a removal with my partner, we found the deceased to be a man who was very well endowed. I mean, this man died on the toilet and his penis was hanging down in the water!

We were putting him on the carrier when my

partner wondered aloud how this man's wife—who stood only about four feet tall—could've possibly accommodated her late husband's huge organ during sex.

"Like this," I said. I then closed my mouth and began poking my tongue against the inside of my cheek, jokingly demonstrating how far up it must've gone inside her.

That got my partner and me really laughing, and it took several minutes for the two of us to regain our composure enough to leave without alerting the widow to our inappropriate behavior.

Wacky
Wakes

Gramps Was No Angel

A woman's father had died, and just before his wake she was at home trying to prepare her two young daughters for the service. This was going to be their first experience with a dead body, and she wanted to make sure both girls knew what to expect.

"You know girls, when you go into the wake room, Gramps is gonna be there," she said.

Both girls nodded their heads and said, "Uh-huh, uh-huh . . ."

Their mother continued, "But he won't be able to see you or say anything to you."

Again, the two girls nodded and said, "Uh-huh, uh-huh . . ."

"But he'll know both of you are there."

Still nodding her head, the older girl looked at her mother and said, "Yes, we know. He'll be up above looking down at us."

The younger girl, however, had a different idea as to where her grandfather was spending eternity, because she suddenly started shaking her head and quickly retorted, "No, he won't. He's gonna be looking up!"

Watch Out For That Caboose . . . It's A Killer

A friend of mine once worked at a funeral home for a rather belligerent funeral director. To illustrate just how bad his boss was, my friend told me the story about a funeral they'd had for a man who died in a massive train wreck.

The widow called my friend's funeral home and told his boss that she wanted to have a wake for her husband. Due to the wreck, the deceased's body was quite mangled, but his boss promised the widow he would do his best to make her husband viewable for the service.

However, when the widow came in before the wake to see her husband's body, she began crying and said, "He looks just awful. That doesn't look a thing like him."

Insulted by her remarks, my friend's boss turned to her and countered, "Well, goddamn it, lady. He didn't die at home in bed, you know. He got hit by 26 train cars *and the caboose!*"

No Shoes, No Service

A member of a local motorcycle gang had been stomped to death by a rival gang, and I happened to be working the front door the night of his wake. This meant that I would stand at the door, open it and greet the people as they came into the funeral home for the service.

It was a strange night—very damp and misty— and the people who came to attend the wake were just as strange. They were a very bizarre group who wore lots of leather and tattoos.

I was afraid that these people might start some trouble, so I told one big burly character attending the wake, "Look, unless you all behave yourselves, I'm gonna shut this thing down."

He told me there wouldn't be any problems and to let him know if anyone got out of line.

Later in the night, I saw a biker chick walking up the front sidewalk. She was wearing a big raccoon coat. Since it was a wet night, the dampened fur smelled foul, like dead rats or something. It was just horrible.

Anyway, I happened to glance down at her feet and notice that she wasn't wearing any shoes under that awful coat. I told her she couldn't come inside without them, and she started to argue with me about it. So I grabbed the big guy and told him about the problem.

He came out, picked her up and threw her onto the front lawn, telling her to come back when she put on some shoes.

As she was picking herself up off the ground, I yelled to her, "*And* a different coat!"

Oh, Brother!

I was working the door at a wake when a man—who appeared to have been drinking—came up to me and wanted to go inside. Since the widow and two sons were in there, I told him I'd let him in but only if he behaved himself. He said he would, and I let him enter the funeral home.

Everything was going along fine until he started yelling for no apparent reason.

I immediately rushed into the room, grabbed him and ushered him out through the back door, reminding him that he had been told to behave himself.

After he left, one of the sons came up to me. He said, "I don't want you to get upset, but that was my mother's brother that you just threw out of here."

I was very embarrassed, and I apologized to him. "I had no idea. I am very sorry—"

"No, don't be. Actually, you did us a favor," he said, interrupting me. "We didn't know how to get rid of him. We wanted him out of here more than you did!"

Peek-A-Boo, I See . . . Steve Jones?

A fellow came into our funeral home to make the funeral arrangements for his recently deceased wife. As we were making them, he told us he wanted to wake and bury her in a negligee because it was what she always wore around their house. We told him we would accommodate his request and would dress her in the negligee for her funeral services.

However, on the night of the wake, we also put a blanket over the front of her body. We had to do this because she was laid out in a full-couch casket, whose whole lid opens up and shows the entire body.

And without a blanket covering her, you could look through the negligee and see everything, including her snapper.

Excuse Me, Where Is The Bar—I Mean—The Bathroom?

My family's funeral home received a lot of requests from families asking for our permission to set up a bar during the hours of their wakes. This was against the law, so we would tell all of them that they couldn't do it.

But this never stopped one particular family whenever they had a funeral at our place.

While they thought we weren't looking, they would turn the men's bathroom into a bar. They'd hide three different types of liquor—vodka, scotch and rye—behind the toilet. And the bottles would never run out because one member of the family had the job of making sure they remained full.

We knew exactly when they opened the bar because there would suddenly be a mad rush to the men's room. Men and women alike would be waiting in line to get into the men's room.

Even though it was against the law, we never stopped them from drinking because they were good customers of ours, and we couldn't afford to lose their business. Besides, we had covered ourselves legally, and what these adults did when they thought we weren't looking really wasn't anybody's business but their own.

Unfortunately, at about 3:45 p.m. of each wake, they would all start to act more like a bunch of rowdy kids than adults. Everyone in the family would become quite drunk by that time, and there'd be at least one fist fight and all of them would have to be thrown out.

Then they'd all go over to the bar across the street until the second set of waking hours began, and it would start all over again.

The Air Conditioned Suit

On the day of his uncle's wake, a nephew dropped off two suits at the funeral home because he wanted me to choose the one his uncle should wear for the service. One suit was blue and the other one was brown. I thought the blue suit would look the best with the casket the family had chosen, so I took it, slit it up the back and put it on his uncle.

The nephew came back a short time later and asked me, "Which suit have you decided to put on my uncle?"

"The blue one," I said.

He said, "Damn. I was hoping you would pick the other one. I wanted to wear the blue suit to the wake."

I said, "I'm sorry, but that's not possible. I already put it on your uncle."

"Can't you just take it off him so I can still wear

it?" he asked.

I said, "Well, yes, I can get it off, but it will be ventilated in the back!"

The nephew resigned himself to wearing the brown suit to his uncle's wake.

Family Fights—The Main Event

There was a fellow in town who had married a very wealthy woman. She died first, but as luck would have it, he died before he inherited any of her money. He passed away only six months after his wife and a few days before her will was to have been read. Our funeral home received the call to handle this man's funeral arrangements.

Ironically, the day of his wake coincided with the day the lawyers opened and read his wife's will. Her will stated that in the event that both she and her husband were dead, everything in her estate was to go to a daughter.

The surviving members of the family consisted of two daughters and four sons, and when the word came down at the wake about their mother's will, the family got into a huge fight. It was a free-for-all between the brothers and the sisters. They were on the floor kicking and punching one another. They even managed to rip the phone out of the wall when one of the siblings wouldn't let go of it.

We finally had to call the police to separate them.

The following day, only the daughter who had been left all the money attended the funeral.

Lying Down On The Job

While making the funeral arrangement for her father, the daughter informed me that she had a very bad back. She said she could only stand for a little while and couldn't sit at all. I offered to put a couch in the receiving line for her to lie on during the wake, but she declined.

Instead, she ended up lying on the floor next to the casket. She had to reach up to shake the hands of those who offered their condolences.

Everyone who came to that wake commented on how strange it was. People were doing a lot of double-takes as they paid their respects.

Return Of The Wanda-ring Dead

There was a nursing home next to the funeral home that I worked for when I was very young. One of the nursing home's permanent residents—a real nut named Wanda—would come to every afternoon wake we were having to pay her respects to the grieving families. She would come over all dressed up, kneel down in front of the casket, say a prayer, speak to the family and then leave when the other people started arriving. She didn't cause any trouble, so we didn't stop her from coming to them.

One particular day, however, she came over a little early for a wake, spoke to the family for a moment and then took a seat next to them in the receiving line. And when the friends of the deceased started to arrive, Wanda stayed right in line with the family, crying up a storm and thanking the people for coming.

Finally, a member of the deceased's family came to me and asked me about this strange woman who was sitting next to them. I told her about Wanda and said I would try to get her to leave.

I went up to Wanda and asked her to come with me, but she insisted that she had to stay with the family. I was young and inexperienced, so I decided it would probably be best to wait for my boss to get back and handle this bizarre situation.

When my boss showed up forty-five minutes later, I told him, "We need to get Wanda out of the funeral home."

"Why?" he asked. "Didn't she just come in and go out?"

"No," I said. "She's sitting with the family in the receiving line."

"Why didn't you grab her and drag her out?"

I told him, "I can't do that to an elderly person. I'm just a kid."

He walked into the wake room and told Wanda to get the heck out of there.

As Wanda came running out, my boss grabbed her by the arm, took her out through the smoking room, out the back door and back to the nursing home. He handed her over to the woman running the nursing home, and he told her not to let Wanda come over to his funeral home again.

But that didn't stop Wanda.

My boss ended up building a stockade fence around his funeral home because she continued to drift over to every wake, just like one of the wandering dead you see in those old horror movies.

No Shoes, No Service: The Shoe Is On The Other Foot

My family's funeral home had three wakes going on at approximately the same time later in the day, and I had scheduled the families to arrive for their wakes in fifteen-minute intervals. The first family was to come in at 1:15 p.m., the second family at 1:30 p.m. and the third at 1:45 p.m. This was done so that my uncle, Tom, could greet all the families as they came in. He was very good with the public relations aspect of the funeral business.

At about 11:30 a.m. as my uncle and I were getting ready for the wakes, my uncle's son came into the funeral home. Uncle Tom took off his shoes, handed them to his son, Tommy Jr., and asked him to go downtown to get them polished.

Tommy Jr. said, "Sure," and left with the shoes.

Well, one o'clock came and went and there wasn't any sign of Tommy Jr.

At 1:15 p.m., the families began arriving, but my uncle couldn't meet any of them because Tommy Jr. still hadn't gotten back with his shoes. He had to stay in the office while I greeted each family, and this made him very angry.

Two o'clock came.

Two-thirty.

Three o'clock.

Three-thirty.

By quarter to four, my uncle's anger had given way to some concern, thinking something might've happened to his son. So he was quite relieved when Tommy Jr. finally came back.

However, his relief lasted all of about ten seconds when he heard why his son had been late.

Instead of waiting around for his father's shoes to be finished, Tommy Jr. told him he had decided to see a double-feature movie while he was downtown.

Waken At A Wake

I was working the front door at a wake when a drunk man came up and informed me he was going inside to attend the service. I tried telling him that it wasn't a wise idea considering his condition, but he said the family wouldn't care and stumbled past me.

The wake proceeded without any problems from this drunk, and I considered myself fortunate. When he suddenly fell sound asleep during the middle of it, I felt as if I had won the lottery.

But as the priest was in the middle of saying the rosary prayers, the drunk suddenly woke up and hollered, "Where the f--- am I?"

Needless to say, that put a quick end to the prayers and to my happy feeling.

Employee Of The Year

Back when I was a funeral director, not many funeral homes in town were willing to do welfare funerals because there wasn't much money in doing them. My funeral home, however, took a funeral no matter how much money was involved, and we always treated these deceased like we treated any others.

We handled one particular welfare case where the deceased was a man who really didn't have anybody or anything. I figure that everybody has to have somebody or something in this world, so I sat down with one of the other guys I worked with and we made up an obituary about him. We included fictional lists of living relatives he was leaving behind and schools he had attended. We also wrote that he was a former employee of—let's say—the Whatjamacallit Company, a company we had also invented.

We submitted the obituary to the newspaper when we were done.

The next day—on the day of this man's wake— we got a call from the personnel director of a business named the Whatjamacallit Company. He said, "Please, you've got to help me. I've been going crazy trying to figure out who this man is whose name appeared in the obituary section. We don't have his name or address or any employment records on him."

I told this man exactly what we had done and how we had pulled the Whatjamacallit name out of the air, never realizing there was a real business by that name.

After I was finished explaining it to him, the personnel director said he thought it was such a nice thing to do for the deceased that he wanted to do something for him, too. So he sent a basket of flowers from the Whatjamacallit Company to this indigent man's wake.

The attached card read: Hope you enjoy your retirement.

A Completed Trip To Heaven?

When a daughter came up to me during her father's wake to inform me the live candle next to his casket had gone out, I immediately congratulated her. I told her that when a candle suddenly goes out by itself during a wake, it signifies that the deceased has just completed his or her trip to Heaven.

She was so happy to hear this that she told the other six members of her family about it. Before the wake was over, each of them came over and thanked me for conveying the good news about their loved one's arrival into Heaven.

The funny thing was, was that I had made up the whole story because I didn't feel like looking around for a match to light the candle.

The Leaning Tower Of "Bella Mia"

My boss and I were working the wake of a deceased whose Italian wife was overacting the part of the grief-stricken widow.

It was so bad that at one point as she stood beside her husband's casket, she began pounding on his chest and started screaming, "Bella Mia . . . Bella Mia," which means "My Beautiful" in Italian. Then she staggered backwards a little bit, collapsed and took out three rows of chairs.

My boss and I stood in the back of the chapel laughing, not knowing what else to do.

Nothing Beats A Great Pair Of Legs

Most wakes are very boring events to work, but I find that it helps me to pass the time by looking at the beautiful women who come in to pay their respects.

At one wake, my attention was immediately drawn to the very beautiful legs of a woman in the deceased's family. She was in the receiving line next to the casket. I spent the next forty-five minutes looking at this woman's legs—they were truly an incredible pair.

When the waking hours were over, she hastily approached me and said, "I've been watching you stare at me for almost an hour, and you didn't even recognize me."

I was very embarrassed by having gotten caught staring at her and also by not recognizing her, but I came back quickly with my reply. "I'm sorry I didn't recognize you, but my eyes never got above your remarkable knees."

She walked out of the funeral home totally confused, wondering whether I deserved to be punched or kissed.

The Great Escape

During my career as a funeral director, I have seen a number of funny things placed in caskets during wakes: golf clubs, decks of cards, bottles of liquor. But the funniest thing ever was a can-opener, which someone had placed in the deceased's hands just in case he needed to get out.

He Was The Life Of The Wake

There was a group of men who would stop by the funeral home at different times of the day to shoot-the-bull with us. One man owned the restaurant across the street. Another was a retired fireman. One was a policeman. And another was Jeff, a man who'd fallen on some hard times and had been out of work for awhile.

One night, Jeff staggered into our funeral home around 6:30 p.m. bombed out of his mind—he was really drunk. He had been out that day celebrating because he'd recently gotten a job at an insurance company and had just made a ton of money by selling a huge policy. So he went out, got loaded and came to tell me about his good fortune.

He also came because he had just heard that the policeman's father had died and wanted to see if it was true or not.

When I told him that the cop's father had indeed died, he asked me to take him to the funeral home where the wake was being held. I really didn't want to take him because he was so drunk. Luckily for me, the restaurant owner—who didn't know Jeff—stopped by because he didn't want to go to the wake alone and was looking for someone to go with him. I told him to take Jeff with him and he did.

About an hour and a half later, the restaurant owner came back and was fuming at me. "You son-of-a-bitch," he said, "I'll never listen to you again."

"What happened?" I asked him.

"What happened? I'll tell you what happened. I got in the car with this guy—who I don't know—and it appears to me that he's had a few too many to drink. But he told me he was okay, so I took him with me. When we got to the funeral home, we went in, signed the register book and waited in line to express our sympathies to the family. We were only about two people away from the casket when, all of a sudden, I heard Jeff go, 'Oooooooh,' and he took a header right into the baskets of flowers next to the casket! They all came tumbling down, and I had to go into the pile to pick him up. They had to stop the wake to put all the flowers back up. And all of this happened because I listened to you!"

The next day, the policeman stopped by our funeral home to tell me that Jeff's drunken flower dive had been the high point of his father's wake.

Terms Of Estrangement

We were trying to arrange the funeral of a woman who was survived by two daughters who hadn't spoken to each other in over twenty years. Because of this rift between the sisters, the family was divided into two factions, which meant we had to deal with both sides individually while making the arrangements for their mother. First, we would talk with one side and then we would talk with the other. Finally, we worked out the details between both.

The wake began at 1:30 p.m., and one of the daughters promptly came in with her side of the family.

At about 2:15 p.m., the other side of the family still hadn't arrived yet. The daughter came out to ask me if I had seen or heard from her sister and the other side of the family.

"I'm sorry, but I haven't," I said.

She said, "I'll bet that no-good-bitch is down rifling through mother's apartment!"

With that, they all got up and left the wake.

A short time later, someone from the family called to say they were down at the apartment and had walked in on the other daughter and her side of the family as they took the things they wanted from the place.

I had to go down there, throw them all out and get a Probate Court order to seal the apartment so we could finish the wake.

What The—?

Just as the afternoon set of calling hours for a wake had concluded, the deceased's widow came up to me and asked if she had time to run down to Probate Court. She wanted to open her late husband's estate before the second set of calling hours began.

I said, "If you run down there right now, you will only be subjecting yourself to public criticism by virtue of your selfish anxiety."

But being the boorish person she was, she paused for a moment, thought about what I had said and then asked, "Would that be a 'yes' or a 'no?'"

Hung Like A Horse—Fly, That Is

I went to a friend's wake to pay my respects, and I was surprised to find the funeral home filled with women who were claiming to be girlfriends of his. My friend had been married, but he had been known to cheat on his wife from time to time. I never knew it had been so rampant, and I was in awe as to the extent of his sexual prowess.

My friend's wife—who had also been well aware of her husband's cheating ways—was just as bewildered by the number of his conquests. She came up to me and asked me how her husband could've been so popular with women.

I remarked, "He must've been hung like a horse."

"He wasn't hung at all. He was only about this big," she said, wiggling her pinky finger at me. "It hardly went inside. Any other ideas?"

I thought about it for a minute and offered, "Maybe they liked to be tickled with it."

Funny
Funerals

THE WIZARD OF ID   Brant parker and Johnny hart

Nothing Gets In The Way Of Progress . . . Or A Funeral

During the morning of a funeral my uncle was conducting, he and the other funeral home's funeral directors were outside. They were lining up the cars that were following in the procession from the funeral home to the church and then onto the cemetery.

All of a sudden, one of the directors dropped dead right in the parking lot as people were coming out to get into their cars. Everybody was so stunned by this man's death that they stood next to their cars in shock, wondering what to do.

My uncle—ever the funeral professional—walked over to the recently deceased, assessed the situation and then put it into perspective by saying, "He's dead. Throw a f---ing sheet over him. We've got a funeral to get out of here."

Lights Are On, But Mom's Not Home

After the services at our funeral home had ended, the widow went up to the casket with the rest of her family to have a final viewing of their loved one. The widow's son was on one side of her and her daughter was on the other.

The widow looked at her husband for a couple of minutes and then turned to her daughter and said, "You know, he hasn't moved an inch since last night."

Both the son and daughter just shook their

heads and said, "Yeah, okay, Mom. Well, whatever." They thought their mother had lost her head for a moment due to the emotional toll of the funeral.

But when their mother reached out, patted their father on the hand and said to her son, "And he's as cold as a cake of ice," the son and daughter quickly hustled her out of the funeral home.

A Grave Setting

Our funeral home had two funerals scheduled for the same day—one at 9 a.m. and the other at 10 a.m.—and both burials also happened to be going to the same cemetery. I was handling the first one and another of our funeral directors was in charge of the second.

Before my funeral started, the children of the deceased told me they wanted to bury their mother with her wedding ring on her finger, so I left it on. But after the funeral was over, the family was waiting for me when I got back to the funeral home and told me that they had changed their minds. They wanted the ring back because they had decided to give it to one of the granddaughters.

I told them that if I could get out to the cemetery before they put the cover on the vault, I could easily get it. Otherwise, it would be a very expensive proposition.

So I jumped back into my car and quickly drove back to the cemetery.

When I arrived at the cemetery, I looked down into the grave and was glad to see that they hadn't put the vault lid on yet. I went down into the grave, unlocked the top of the casket, reached in and got the wedding ring.

As I was scrambling up out of the grave, my partner—who was leading the second funeral into the cemetery—saw me coming up. He was so shocked by the sight of me crawling out of the ground that he almost drove his car off the road.

I was afraid the family might have the same reaction if they saw where I had been and decided to go back down into the grave until they passed by me. But the other grave was so close to the one I was in that I had to stay down until they finished the committal service, loaded all the cars and left the cemetery.

No Deposit, No Return

A member of a local motorcycle gang had died, and members of different motorcycle clubs from all over the country came to his funeral—even the Hell's Angels from California.

There were fifty motorcycles participating in the procession from the church to the cemetery. The six pall bearers were even riding motorcycles. They were in front of the hearse doing wheelies all the way through town.

After the committal at the cemetery, all the motorcyclists opened up some coolers, grabbed cans of cold beer, toasted the deceased and then threw the empties into his grave.

I See London, I See France

Just before a graveside committal service, the priest doing it called me over to him. He was standing away from everyone, holding his Bible down in front of himself and looking very distressed.

I rushed over to him and asked, "What's the matter, Father?"

He looked down at himself, then at me and said, "Do me a favor for the committal. Stand me behind a monument or something because my fly is busted, and I can't get it closed."

Ready . . . Aim . . . Duck!

The funeral home I worked at hired a certain National Guard firing squad for every military funeral we were conducting. We used them so often that I became rather friendly with the sergeant who was in charge.

Whenever we used the squad, I would always tease him about how bad they were by telling him, "Try to have your people synchronized this time so they all fire their guns at the same time. Not 'bing, bang, boom, bong,' all with different timing. Try to get them to hit them all together."

When he was ready to give the signal for the

squad to open fire, I would always manage to find a big monument to stand near. Then I would catch his eye by ducking behind the monument, pretending I was afraid of being shot by those guys if I stayed out in the open.

The sergeant would see me trying to hide and he'd start laughing. Then you'd hear, "bing, bang, boom, bong," because he would be laughing so hard that he'd give the wrong command.

She Needed A Hand . . . Literally

After a winter graveside committal service ended, I began loading the family into our Cadillac limousine. It was very slippery out, and I wanted to make sure everyone got into the limo okay.

I was helping the deceased's daughter get into the back of the limo when I suddenly slipped on a snow bank and went sliding down. Trying to stop my fall, I grabbed hold of the door. But instead of stopping, I kept sliding down until I slid completely underneath the limo, taking the door with me and accidentally slamming it on the daughter's hand.

I screamed for someone to open the door, but the man driving the limousine had it in gear, which causes the doors of a Cadillac to automatically lock. So the driver crawled over the front seat and everyone in his way to the back of the limo, trying to lift up the lock button but failing because the car was still in gear. He couldn't figure out why the locks wouldn't go up.

By this time, the daughter was screaming and I was lying underneath the car up to my chest in mud and wet snow, having just slammed a car door onto the hand of the deceased's daughter.

Fortunately for the daughter—and my funeral home, considering the frequency of lawsuits these days—she wasn't seriously injured.

Keep On Truckin'

A local fire chief died and a huge fanfare was planned for his funeral. The plans included music from a band, attendance by many of his fellow firemen from stations around the state and his body being transported to the church service on top of a fire truck.

Anyway, when the fire truck arrived with the body at the church, I told a coworker to get our church truck—the rolling support device a casket is put on so it can be easily moved inside church.

"You mean you didn't bring it?" he asked.

My heart jumped into my throat and my first thought was, *Here I've got well over one hundred volunteer firemen on hand and a band of bagpipes playing music. What are we gonna do? Have the pall bearers stand and hold the casket for the entire forty minutes of Mass?*

Luckily, someone called the funeral home and the station wagon taking the flowers to the cemetery hadn't left yet. The two men in charge of the flowers said they would put a church truck in the wagon and bring it out to us.

As one of my coworkers was telling me that the church truck was on its way, I saw two seventy-year-old men driving our station wagon up the street. They were going about eighty miles an hour, their faces pulled back tight from the G-force.

Then they slammed on the brakes, dropped off the church truck, and sped off to the cemetery like our funeral home had planned it that way all along.

They Got The Limousine For A Steal

We were conducting a funeral service at a church in a bad section of town. This neighborhood was always being reported about in the newspaper because of all the drug deals, murders and thefts that occurred there.

As we were leaving church to take the funeral to the cemetery for the burial, I looked over to see the pall bearers' limousine drive out of the parking lot. I thought someone was only moving it until I noticed that our limo driver was standing next to me.

In a panic, I said to him, "Johnny . . . the car!"

Johnny looked over, saw it speeding away and yelled at the top of his lungs, "Oh, shit! Somebody's stealing the limo!"

I asked him what we were going to do, and Johnny replied, "Be grateful that they didn't take the hearse. At least we won't have to carry the casket over to the cemetery."

Pick A Cemetery, Any Cemetery

I was leading a funeral procession and we were supposed to be going to St. Paul's Cemetery for the burial. However, I had just returned from vacation and forgot to ask which cemetery we were going to. So I led the procession over to St. Peter's Cemetery— the place where I thought it was being held.

As I was driving into St. Peter's, the sexton at the cemetery was standing by the entrance and said to me, "Dick, you're at the wrong cemetery. You're supposed to be at *St. Paul's* Cemetery."

I said, "Thank you," and then drove around in a complete circle, exited the cemetery and went over to St. Paul's.

The family was very decent about the mix-up. Actually, they thought the whole thing was rather hilarious.

Nun Of The Cars Were Moving

A nun's mother passed away and groups of nuns from convents throughout New England came to attend the funeral. The daughter was stationed in New Jersey at the time, and her convent sent up a delegation of about five cars full of nuns for the service.

When we were getting ready to leave the funeral home for church, I called out the names of the groups of nuns. They were to pay their final respects to the deceased, go outside, get into their cars and follow the funeral procession to the church. But when I went outside, I saw that none of their cars were following the lead car and the hearse as they pulled out of the driveway.

I ran up to the nun sitting behind the wheel of the head car and quickly explained to her that she had to move along. If she didn't, she and the other cars in procession wouldn't be able to follow the funeral home's cars to the church and would get lost.

She turned to me and unexpectedly said, "I don't know how to start the car."

Stunned by this revelation, I asked, "Didn't you just drive this car three hours from New Jersey?"

She told me she had, but someone else had started the car for her in New Jersey—her strong points were stopping and steering.

Not knowing what else to do in this crazy situation, I got her out of the car. Then I got in, started it, got back out and put her in again.

I held my breath as I watched her drive off.

That's Not Jet Lag He's Suffering From

A widow handed me fifteen dollars during her husband's wake. She asked me to buy a quart of bourbon and to place it inside the closed lower end of the casket. After the wake ended, I did as she had asked.

On the morning of the funeral, the widow insisted that the lower end of the casket be opened.

When I asked why she wanted to check her husband's casket, she said to me, "I just want to make certain he has his favorite drink on his trip to Heaven."

The Best Laid Plans Of Mice & Funeral Directors

Because I am not Jewish, my funeral home doesn't get to handle many Jewish funerals. Once, however, a member of a Jewish family in town—a very old industrial family—had died, and they asked me to handle the funeral.

The burial was going to take place in a Jewish cemetery about sixty miles away from us, so I called the cemetery and made arrangements with them for the burial. This included having a police motorcycle escort meet our fifteen car procession at the town line to lead us to the cemetery.

On the day of the funeral, the police escort met us on the edge of town and took us to a small rectangular shaped cemetery that had only one road leading into it and out of it.

As we followed our escort into the cemetery, I began shitting nickels, thinking to myself, *Oh, God. Now what the hell?* I looked for the tent to locate the open grave, but there wasn't one. And as we went further into the cemetery, I could see that not only wasn't there a tent, but there also wasn't an open grave or anybody who worked for the cemetery anywhere in sight. I was getting nervous because we had never been to this cemetery before, and it looked as if they might've forgotten that we were even coming.

When I reached the middle of the cemetery, I looked for the motorcycle cop and saw that he had proceeded completely through the cemetery and was waiting for us at the exit. He motioned for me to keep going through the cemetery until I exited it, too. Because it couldn't get any worse, I took the whole procession through the cemetery and out of it.

He then led the funeral procession down a few more blocks to another Jewish cemetery that had a tent and an open grave in it.

What had happened was that this town had both a "new" Jewish cemetery and an "old" Jewish cemetery. The police escort had assumed it was the new cemetery because that was where everybody was being buried these days. This, however, was an old Jewish family who still had graves available in an old family plot.

Before I could tell the family how sorry I was for the mix-up, a few of its members came up to me and said, "Now that was really something."

"You're right about that," I reluctantly agreed.

I was getting ready to explain the problem to them when one of them said to me, "You know, that was so nice of you to take Harry past his sister Hazel's grave like that. We've never seen that done before, but that was so nice. Your funeral home has thought of everything."

I decided it was best to keep my mouth shut.

Honey, Did You Forget Your Bra Or Are You Just Happy To See Me?

One morning, a couple in their 30s exited from their car and began making their way up the front steps to the funeral home to attend a funeral service. But when they got halfway up, the wife suddenly stopped dead in her tracks, grabbed her husband and whispered nervously in his ear. Then she finished climbing the stairs and went inside the funeral home while he turned and quickly came back down.

The husband mentioned something to us about having to go home momentarily because his wife had forgotten something. Then he drove off in a hurry.

There were three of us standing outside when the husband returned fifteen minutes later. And as we watched him hustle back up to the funeral home, we all burst into laughter.

As he ran up the steps, his wife's brassiere could be seen hanging all the way down the side of his coat and trousers. It had somehow managed to fall out of his coat pocket and was held in place by one of the bra's hooks, which had gotten hung up on the pocket.

Oh, to have been inside the funeral home when he waltzed in through the front door!

You'll Shoot Your Ear Off

During one military funeral we were having, I sent the funeral procession out to the cemetery ahead of me. I entered the cemetery a short while later to find the line of cars sitting along the side of the road. They were waiting for me to arrive and lead them to the grave.

However, as I was about to pass the limousine containing the members of the National Guard's firing squad, a big bubble suddenly formed in the limo's roof. All four doors flew open and everyone scrambled to get out, their hands covering their ears.

What happened was one of the guys in the firing squad had been playing with the strap on his rifle and had somehow hit the trigger, which caused the rifle to discharge inside the limo.

They were all deaf for three days afterwards.

Tons Of Fun

On the morning of a funeral for a woman we were burying, I had sent one of our limousines to pick up the three daughters of the deceased. One of the daughters weighed about 350 pounds and had a very stiff knee, making it even harder for her to exit the back of a limo, so I told the driver before he left that he should put her in the front seat. But when the limo returned, he had obviously forgotten my instructions because all three daughters were seated in the back.

I knew there would be a problem in getting the heavy sister out, so I took it upon myself to help. One of the two slimmer sisters got out and tried to pull the heavy sister out of the back seat, and I went around to the other side, got in and began pushing the heavy one from her backside. Just one of her cheeks was the size of me, but I pushed with all I had.

When the slim sister who was pulling from the other side saw what I was doing, she began to laugh hysterically and let go. The heavy sister fell back on top of me, nearly crushing me to death, and all of us began laughing over our predicament.

It finally took about five minutes to get the heavy sister out of the limo.

During that time, the people who were arriving for the funeral were in quite an uproar, laughing at our "Three Stooges" act in the back seat of the limousine.

An En-Lightning Experience

We were at a graveside committal service about ready to begin the prayers when, all of a sudden, a dark cloud came up on us.

The priest had just begun reciting *The Lord's Prayer*, only managing to say, "Our Father—" when a bolt of lightning struck the ground and forced him to improvise the rest of the prayer. "Our Father . . . it looks like there's going to be a storm, and we'd better get the heck out of here!"

Have You Hugged A Monument Today?

One very snowy day, we were bringing a funeral into a cemetery for a burial service on the top of a very big hill.

The only way to get to the grave was by walking up a steep incline, but it went much easier under the supervision of the cemetery's sexton. The sexton at this cemetery was named Burt, and Burt was a man who liked to be tipped for his help. If you wanted good service, you had to give him a few dollars. But because my boss was against tipping him, we never gave him anything. So when Burt noticed another funeral home—a generous one that always slipped him ten dollars—bringing a funeral into the cemetery right behind us, he bypassed us and offered his help to the other funeral, leaving us to navigate the incline alone.

I don't know how we did it without Burt's assistance, but we managed to carry the casket up the hill. I was on the back, my partner was on the front and the six hired pall bearers were on the two sides.

We were walking across the wooden planks and were just about ready to set it down on the lowering device when everything shifted—the fake grass, the planking, the lowering device, everything. Now, hired pall bearers never get hurt because they always let go of the casket at the first sign of any trouble, so all of these guys disappeared. This left me holding one end and my partner holding the other to keep the casket from dropping into the grave.

Down below, the sexton had his mouth wide open in disbelief while the family managed to scream, "Oh, my God . . . Oh, my God . . ."

My partner—a rather large individual with an ego of even bigger proportions—wrapped his free arm around a nearby monument, looked down at them and informed them, "No need to worry. I have everything under control."

Sister Dearest

We had a funeral involving the death of one of two elderly sisters who hadn't spoken to one another in over twenty-five years. These two sisters had absolutely hated each other, but you would've never known it from the funeral. During the three day span, the surviving sister cried and moaned and carried on as if she had just lost her best friend.

Each time someone got up from the kneeler at the wake, she'd go up to her sister's casket and moan, "Oh, my precious sister. I miss you so much that I can't live my life without you."

Her sobbing and moaning carried over to the church.

At the cemetery, just as the priest had started the committal service, the sister started moaning again, saying, "Oh, sister. I miss you so much that I can't live my life without you. I'm going to jump into the grave! I'm going to jump into the grave with you!"

The priest got two minutes into the committal before he finally grew tired of her pretentious display.

He suddenly stopped and said to this woman who was over seventy years old, "Young lady, I have listened to you at the funeral home. I have listened to you during the Mass. Would you please do us all a favor? If you are going to jump into the grave, please do it now so I can go on with the service."

A roar of laughter rose in the background, but the sister stood there in shock, not knowing what to do.

The priest then asked her for permission to restart the committal. When she didn't say anything, he continued.

After the service, the priest went over to the family to express his condolences. As he did, there was a loud shriek and the elderly sister fell to the ground. But the priest ignored her, stepping over her body as he walked down the line of family members and shook their hands.

When the priest got into his car and left the cemetery, everybody else followed his lead, leaving this woman lying there.

A short while later, she lifted her head off the ground and was surprised to find that there wasn't anybody left at her sister's grave to help her. So she finally got up, dusted herself off, got into her car and drove off.

Just Following Orders, General

I spent a number of years working at my family's funeral home. As a boss, my father was a very punctual, very regimented man who reminded me more of a military general than an employer. This was very obvious during a funeral we were conducting for a priest. My father ran that priest's funeral just like it was a military operation, spitting out orders that were to be carried out immediately without question.

For this funeral my father made it perfectly clear to me that I had to be at the church rectory at exactly one o'clock. I figured out how much time it would take me to back the hearse out of the garage, pull it up to the door, load the casket into it, leave for the rectory and still have enough time to be there by one o'clock.

I was right on schedule—having just backed the hearse out of the garage—when my father drove up, got out of his car and yelled to me, "Get in the hearse and drive!"

My father got into the hearse with me, and we left the funeral home.

We were halfway to the rectory before my father looked behind him and asked in a panic, "Where's the goddamn casket?"

I looked at him and said, "It's still at the funeral home. You told me to get in the hearse and drive, and that's exactly what I did."

He went crazy!

I Smell A Refund!

During a very busy stretch of funerals in our town, a friend of mine died and it was his wish to be buried by my family's funeral home. However, his two surviving sisters didn't want to use our funeral home. They didn't like my family and didn't want anything to do with us. But they respected their brother's wishes and came to our funeral home, anyway.

From the beginning, nothing about the funeral was right. The sisters found fault with everything we did, and they made sure *everything* we did seemed wrong. Luckily, we made it through the wake, the Mass, and the trip to the cemetery with only a few minor complaints.

It was at the cemetery where all hell broke loose.

The important thing to know here is that during heavy periods of funerals, priests will usually rely on reading the deceased's vault cover in order to recall the name of the person being buried. Then they don't have to memorize every name for every committal service they perform.

So the priest started his graveside prayers by saying, "We would like to remember our dearly departed—" And as he was about to read the name off the vault cover, I glanced over and realized that the wrong name was on it. Instead of Joe Blow, it said Sally Schmally. Like a slow motion nightmare, before I could stop the priest from reading aloud the wrong name and save my neck, he said, "—sister, Sally Schmally."

Both sisters started screaming for a refund.

The funniest thing about that funeral, though, was the reaction by the man from the vault company who had been standing off to the side. As soon as he realized the wrong name was on the vault cover, he went absolutely nuts and took off out of the cemetery quicker than a bat out of Hell. In some other cemetery in town, some other priest on some other funeral was about to read Joe Blow's name off the wrong vault cover during the committal.

Going For A Swim, Esther?

I was reading aloud the names on the car list for the procession to church. Most of the names I was calling out were nurses. As I looked at the names before saying them, I realized that I knew many of these women.

One of the names I was about to call out was a nurse I knew very well by the name of Esther White. Trying to be a big shot, I said very vociferously, "Miss Esther Williams," instead of Esther White. For some reason I was thinking about the famous swimmer.

Well, the whole place went into an uproar and

everyone started laughing. I wanted to bury my head in the sand someplace. I didn't even want to go on with this funeral.

When Esther walked by me on the way to her car, she said in a voice loud enough for everyone to hear, "And I can't even swim!"

How Do I Spell Embarrassed? S-M-I-T-H

While I was outside taking down names for the list of cars going on the funeral, a girl I once knew got out of her car and walked up the sidewalk towards me. I immediately recognized her because I had gone to high school with her. However, it had been ten years since we'd graduated, and I couldn't remember her last name.

She came up to me and said, "Hi, Bob. How are you?"

"I'm good, Jane," I said. "How about you?"

She said, "I'm fine, thanks."

Needing to put her name on the car list but too embarrassed to let her know I couldn't remember it, I stood there awkwardly for a few seconds until it dawned on me how I could painlessly get it out of her.

I asked, "Jane, just so it's announced correctly when it's time to leave for church, how do you spell your last name?"

However, she dashed my resourcefulness by informing me, "How do I spell my last name? How about just like everyone else with the same name spells it: S-M-I-T-H!"

Pain In The Mouth

An elderly lady had passed away, leaving two daughters as her immediate survivors. One of the daughters was married and the other was a spinster.

The daughters got along very well, but the husband of the married one really hated his sister-in-law. According to him, she was good for nothing but complaining. She complained constantly and she complained about everything. In fact, he made it a point to tell each of us working on the funeral that all his sister-in-law could do was bitch.

All of us soon learned he wasn't exaggerating.

When the limousine bringing the three of them to the church finally arrived, the spinster's mouth was already in gear. She got out of the limo complaining about the dismal weather we were experiencing that morning.

However, she was finally forced to stop her griping when she stumbled while walking up to church and struck her mouth against the edge of one of the steps. She cut her lip and blood could be seen pouring down her chin.

Several of us from the funeral home ran to assist her, but her brother-in-law—not one to hide his dislike for this woman—stopped us by extending his right hand like a school crossing guard stopping traffic.

Then he uttered loudly enough for all to hear, "That ought to keep her goddamn mouth shut!"

Hilarious
Headstones

NON SEQUITUR   By Wiley

Reader, pass on!—don't waste your time
On bad biography and bitter rhyme;
For what I am, this crumbling clay insures,
And what I was, is no affair of yours!
— *Tombstone in New Jersey*

We must all die, there is no doubt;
Your glass is running—mine is out.
— *Shoreditch Churchyard*

Sacred to the memory of ANTHONY DRAKE,
Who died for peace and quietness sake;
His wife was constantly scolding and scoffin',
So he sought for repose in a twelve-dollar coffin.
— *Burlington Churchyard, Mass.*

This tombstone is a Milestone;
Hah! how so?
Because beneath lies MILES who's
MILES below.
— *Webley Churchyard, Yorks*

This spot is the sweetest I've seen in my life,
For it raises my flowers and covers my wife.
— *Churchyard in Wales*

Here lies entombed old ROGER NORTON,
Whose sudden death was oddly brought on;
Trying one day his corn to mow off,
The razor slipped and cut his toe off.
The toe, or rather what it grew to,
An inflammation quickly flew to;
The part affected took to mortifying,
And poor old ROGER took to dying.
— *Quordon, England*

This stone was raised by SARAH'S lord,
Not SARAH'S virtues to record,—
For they're well-known to all the town,—
But it was *raised* to keep *her down.*
— *Kilmury Churchyard*

Beneath these stones repose the bones
Of THEODOSIUS GRIMM,
He toak his beer from year to year,
And then his bier took him.
— *Durham Churchyard, England*

Here lies the body of MARY ANN LOWDER;
She burst whilst drinking a seidlitz powder;
Called from this world to her heavenly rest,
She should have waited till it effervesced.
— *Burlington Churchyard, Mass.*

Here lies poor
But honest BRYAN TUNSTAL;
He was a most expert angler
Until Death, envious of his merit,
Threw out his line,
Hooked him,
And landed him here
The 21st day of April, 1790.
— *Minster Churchyard, Yorkshire*

Here lie I, and no wonder I am dead,
For the wheel of a wagon went over my head.
— *Churchyard in Pembrokeshire*

Poor MARTHA SHIELL has gone away,
Her would if she could, but her couldn't stay;
Her had 2 bad legs and a baddish cough,
It was her two bad legs that carried her off.
— *Gravestone near London*

Here lies the body of poor FRANK ROW,
Parish clerk, and gravestone cutter.
And this is writ to let you know,
What FRANK for others us'd to do,
Is now for FRANK done by another.
— *Shelby Churchyard, Yorkshire*

Here doth lye the bodie
Of JOHN FLYE, who did die
By a stroke from a sky-rocket
Which hit him on the eye-socket.
— *Durness Churchyard, Sutherlandshire*

Here lies the body of ANN MANN;
Who lived an old woman,
And died and old MANN.
— *Bath Abbey*

Life is a jest and all things show it;
I thought so once but now I know it.
— *Westminster Abbey, London*

The Lord saw good, I was lopping off wood,
And down fell me from the tree;
I met with a check, and I broke my neck,
And so death lopped off me.
— *Quordon, England*

Here lies my wife in earthy mould,
Who, when she liv'd did naught but scold;
Peace, wake her not, for now she's still,
She had, but now I have my will.
— *Ellon Churchyard*

Grim death took me without any warning, I was
well at night, and dead at nine in the morning.
— *Churchyard of Sevenoaks, Kent*

To all my friends I bid adieu;
A more sudden death you never knew:
As I was leading the old mare to drink,
She kicked and killed me quicker'n a wink.
— *Oxford, N.H.*

Against his will
Here lies GEORGE HILL
Who from a cliff
Fell down quite stiff;
When it happened is not known,
Therefore not mention'd on this stone.
— *Churchyard in Isle of Thanet*

Her lies one MORE, and no *More* than he:
One *More* and no *More*! how can that be?
Why one *More* and no *More* may well be here alone
But here lies one *More*, and that's *More* than one.
— *St. Bennet's, Paul's Wharf, London*

Tears cannot restore her—therefore I weep.
— *New Hampshire*

Here lies the man RICHARD,
And MARY his wife;
Their surname was PRICHARD,
They lived without strife;
And the reason was plain—
They abounded in riches,
They no care had, nor pain,
And the *wife wore the breeches.*
— *Essex, England*

Anchored at last.
— *Naugatuck, Conn.*

Here lies me and my three daughters,
Brought here by using Siedlitz waters;
If we had stuck to Epsom salts,
We wouldn't have been in these here vaults.
— *Childwald, England*

Here lieth W. W.
Who never more will trouble you, trouble you.
— *Lambeth Churchyard*

It *is* humid.
— *On the headstone of Ronnie Shakes*

I WANT YOU

to tell Edward Bergin YOUR funny funeral home story! Here is your chance to have your humorous encounter with death immortalized in an all-new, future edition of his book entitled *The Definitive Guide To Underground Humor II: Digging Deeper*. Just submit your story in writing to Edward Bergin (c/o OFFbeat Publishing, P.O. Box 735, Waterbury, CT 06720-0735) for consideration. If he includes your story, you will receive 5 autographed copies and the undying laughter of readers everywhere.

ORDER FORM

YES! Please send me _____ autographed copies of the book
The Definitive Guide To Underground Humor @ $8.95 each $ _____

6% Sales Tax (CT only) $ _____

Subtotal $ _____

Orders shipping to USA and Canada only   Shipping & Handling $ __3.00__
 For foreign orders, please call us for rates

TOTAL $ _____

Payment Method (Please Remit in US Funds):
❏ Check or Money Order made payable in full to OFFbeat Publishing
❏ Please charge my ❏ VISA ❏ MasterCard ❏ American Express
   ❏ Optima ❏ Discover

Card # _____ Exp. Date ____ / ____

Signature _____

Shipping Address (Please Print or Type):

Name _____ Phone _____

Address _____

City _____ State _____ Zip Code _____

Postal Orders: Complete this order form and mail it to OFFbeat Publishing,
P.O. Box 735, Waterbury, CT 06720-0735

FAX Orders: Complete this order form and FAX it to (203) 755-8178

To Order By Phone, Call Toll Free
1-800-757-5107
From 9 am to 5 pm EST